EARTHWORMS
OF THE GREAT LAKES

By Cindy Hale

Kollath+Stensaas
PUBLISHING

Kollath+Stensaas Publishing
394 Lake Avenue South, Suite 406
Duluth, MN 55802
Office: 218.727.1731
info@kollathstensaas.com
www.kollathstensaas.com

EARTHWORMS *of the* GREAT LAKES

Printed in the United States of America
10 9 8 7 6 5 4 3 2 1 0 Second Edition

ISBN-13: 978-1-936571-05-5

Cover photo by Steve Mortensen, all other photos by Erik Hahn
Illustrations by Rick Kollath and Rachel Makarral
Graphic Design by Rick Kollath

TABLE OF CONTENTS

ACKNOWLEDGEMENTS

This book would never have been conceived were it not for the support of Drs. Lee Frelich, Peter Reich and John Moriarity. When nobody else wanted to believe the story that was unfolding, they provided moral and financial support that convinced me to pursue this crazy line of research. Special thanks go out to Dr. John Pastor, my first true mentor.

Over the years, there have been dozens of undergraduate and graduate students who contributed to the work upon which this book is based; thanks to each and every one of them! Especially for not giving up when backs hurt from carrying hundreds of gallons of water into the field sites under conditions nothing short of nasty: too hot, buggy, cold or wet. You name it, we lived through it.

On a more personal note, thanks go out to my family. My mom, a one woman pep squad, who never tires of telling everyone how proud she is of her daughter. My siblings who know I'm crazy but love me anyway. My husband Jeff, who provides me with the love and support I need to keep myself sane and regain perspective when things get crazy. My daughter May, whose joyous face reminds me everyday why I should care about the future. May's birth parents, for giving us the gift of life itself. Finally, thanks to my dad whose spirit lives in everything I do and who first hooked me on the wonders of nature through his own unabashed love of all things living and growing.

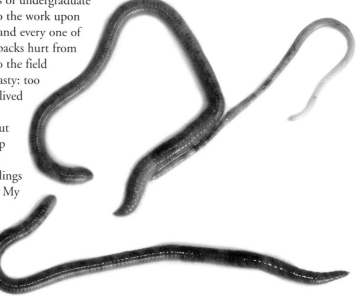

EARTHWORMS, AN INTRODUCTION

Why should I be interested in earthworms?

Earthworms are the ultimate "ecosystem engineers." They change the fundamental processes of an ecosystem through their feeding and burrowing activities and in so doing are changing the face of hardwood forests across the Great Lakes region. Many of the much beloved native forest plants such as trilliums, orchids and other spring and summer flowering plants can disappear following earthworm invasion, and regeneration of sugar maple trees themselves may be threatened.

Learning about earthworms and how they affect forest ecosystems can also give you rare insight into how ecosystems work and how non-native species make their mark as they invade new places around the globe. Once you become aware of non-native earthworms and their impacts, you will begin to notice the signs of invasion (or non-invasion) as you explore the forests and other ecosystems of the Great Lakes and perhaps, become interested in helping to preserve and protect earthworm-free areas across the region.

Native vs. non-native

No native earthworm species have been documented in the Great Lakes region of North America. Any native North American species of earthworms (in the family *Megascolecidae*) that may have been living in the region were likely extirpated when glacial ice sheets covered the Upper Midwest 11,000 to 14,000 years ago, leaving the glaciated areas of North America earthworm-free.

Natural colonization by earthworms (native or non-native) happens very slowly, with earthworms spreading less than one-half mile in 100 years. So, forests of the Great Lakes region developed in the complete absence of earthworms. For thousands of years, no earthworms existed in this region until European settlers began arriving around the mid-1800s.

All of the earthworms you have come to know and love in the Great Lakes region are non-native; most are European (in the family *Lumbricidae*) and initially arrived with European settlement. But they continue to be transported, intentionally and unintentionally, through a range of human activities such as the dumping of unused fishing bait, transport of compost and mulch, and anything else that moves soil.

The suite of 16 earthworm species you will find in this guide includes a group of species invading not only North America, but all around the globe. Although there are 3,000 to 4,000 earthworm species globally, this select group of earthworm species turns out to be good

This map shows the extent of Glaciation throughout North American. Any native earthworm species in the glaciated areas would've been eradicated.

Area of Glaciation

invaders. They can tolerate a wider range of environmental conditions and are well adapted to being moved around, intentionally and unintentionally, by humans. The combination of being good colonizers and "ecosystem engineers" sets the stage for earthworms to have major impacts across regions they invade.

How did they get here?

The first earthworms probably arrived with soils and plants brought from Europe. Ships traveling to North America used rocks and soil as ballast, which they dumped on shore as they adjusted the ballast weight of the ship. During the late 1800s and early 1900s many European settlers imported European plants for both crop and ornamental gardens that likely had earthworms or earthworm cocoons (egg cases) in their soils. As a result, non-native earthworms have been around since European settlement. Perhaps that's why so many of us believe that earthworms have always been here.

Approximately 110 million dollars worth of earthworms are imported by the U.S. each year from Canada for the fishing bait industry, and they are all foreigners to this continent! The widespread use of earthworms as fishing bait is an important contributor to the spread of earthworms around the Great Lakes. Advancing edges of earthworm invasion often radiate from lakeshores, fishing resorts, boat landings and road ditches. All common bait worms are non-native species. When anglers dump unused fishing bait on the land or water, they are introducing an non-native species.

MYTH BUSTER: Earthworms *can* live in water for many months because they "breathe" through their skin (though they probably don't prefer it). It's better to throw unused bait in the trash!

Additionally, earthworms can be unintentionally moved by anything that moves soil. Earthworm cocoons (egg cases) are particularly easy to move inadvertently because they are small, hard to see and can tolerate more extreme temperatures and drying than the earthworms themselves. Both earthworms and their cocoons can be transported via:

➢ *Compost, leaf mulch and topsoil.*

➢ *Landscape plants or trees with soil around their roots.*

➢ *Road building that involves bringing in soils from elsewhere.*

➢ *Vehicles with tire treads that carry soil including construction, farming and logging equipment, all-terrain vehicles and mountain bikes.*

Are non-native earthworms everywhere?

No. Although earthworms have been in the Great Lakes region for a long time, they are not everywhere. Areas where human activity has been the most intense for the longest period of time, have the highest probability of being invaded by earthworms. However, some large earthworm-free areas still exist, especially in the more remote areas of our region, and ongoing invasions are occurring in many areas through both the natural spread of established populations and with the continued aid of humans. Without humans moving them around, earthworms move slowly. If we stop introducing them we can retain earthworm-free areas for a long time. Even in areas where some earthworms are already present, we want to take precautions to prevent introducing any more non-native earthworm species. All common non-native earthworm species are not everywhere. There are some new non-native earthworms such as the Asian earthworms in the genus *Amynthas* becoming available for sale (especially for composting) that could have even more harmful effects.

What can I do?

Unlike many non-native plant species that can be dispersed by the wind or animals, earthworms are spread primarily by human activities. So even simple actions on your part can make a big difference when it comes to containing the spread of non-native earthworms!

You can help…

Spread the word. Tell others "the dirt" on invasive earthworms in the Great Lakes region. Download the FAQ sheet and poster from our website: www.greatlakeswormwatch.org

Prevent introductions of earthworms to any site by avoiding activities that we know spread earthworms:

➤ If you use earthworms as fishing bait, throw any unused earthworms in the trash, not in the water or on land.

➤ If you use earthworms for composting, before you use the compost, freeze it solid for at least one week (a month is better). This kills the earthworms as well as their egg cases (cocoons) which are often more tolerant of drying and freezing than the earthworms themselves. If you live in an area that gets sub-freezing temps for at least a month straight each winter, you can do this by putting a bucket of the compost in an unheated building.

➤ Do not transport leaves, mulch, compost or soil from one place to another unless you are confident that there are no earthworms or their cocoons present.

➤ If you use ATVs or other vehicles with tire treads that can hold soil, be sure to wash all soil from treads before transporting the vehicle from one place to another.

➤ Join the Great Lakes Worm Watch citizen science effort by:
   • Documenting earthworm occurrences in your area.
   • Learning to identify different earthworm species.
   • Conducting earthworm, soil or habitat surveys to add to our growing citizen science database.

If non-native earthworms are already in an area what can I do?

Once earthworms become established there is no known way to remove them, so prevention is the best protection at this point. But just because one or even a few earthworm species are present in a site, that doesn't mean all potential earthworms are present. Research clearly shows that the more species of earthworms found in a site, the greater the potential impacts, especially to native plant species. This is because different earthworms have different feeding and burrowing behaviors and the synergistic effects when multiple earthworm species are present is greater than the sum of the effects of the individual species. There are several species of earthworms that are not yet widespread across the Great Lakes region but have the potential to be very destructive. Doing what you can to help prevent further introductions can make a big difference.

IMPACTS *of the* EARTHWORM INVASION

Ask anyone on the street if earthworms are good for ecosystems and you will undoubtedly receive a resounding, "YES!" When asked why, they may say something like, "earthworms mix and aerate the soil." It's a basic ecological concept that we may have learned as early as kindergarten. However, recent research on the invasions of these seemingly benevolent creatures into previously earthworm-free hardwood forests of the Great Lakes region has seriously challenged that belief. Researchers have documented dramatic changes in native hardwood forest ecosystems when non-native earthworms invade, including losses of native understory plant species and tree seedlings, changes in soil structure and declines in nutrient availability. There is also fascinating evidence emerging that changes caused by non-native earthworms may lead to a cascade of other changes in the forest that affect populations of small mammals, birds and amphibians, exacerbate the impacts of herbivores like white-tailed deer and facilitate invasions of other non-native species such as slugs, European buckthorn and garlic mustard. These results suggest that non-native earthworms may pose a grave threat to the biodiversity and long term stability of hardwood forest ecosystems in the region.

But how can this be? How can a group of organisms previously thought to be so good for ecosystems, now seem to be so bad? The reality is that all the good things you have heard about earthworms have largely come from their effects in human-dominated systems like gardens and farm fields where they were first described as "ecosystem engineers." An ecosystem engineer is a species that actually creates and modifies a habitat, affecting some of the most fundamental processes in an ecosystem (like decomposition and nutrient cycling). Their effects on those processes cascade

Sugar maple forests before earthworm invasion usually have high diversity of native understory plants and tree seedlings with total understory plant cover of 75 to 100 percent.

Sugar maple forests after earthworm invasion often experience dramatic declines in plant species diversity, tree seedling regeneration and total understory plant cover can drop below 25 percent.

throughout all other parts of the ecosystem. Earthworms are "beavers of the soil," altering the soil's very structure and chemistry. The same mixing and breaking up of organic material that helps increase aeration, water infiltration and fertility in gardens and farm fields has very different effects in previously earthworm-free hardwood forests, because earthworms change the ecological "ground rules" that have been in place in forests for thousands of years.

In previously earthworm-free hardwood forests, decomposition of the tons of leaf litter produced each year is controlled by the actions of fungi and bacteria. Lacking a powerful detrivore (something that consumes disintegrating leafy material) such as earthworms, decomposition is slower than the accumulation of new litter and the result is the formation of a thick, spongy forest floor, often called a "duff layer." The duff layer can be up to 10 cm (4 or 5 inches) thick in forests dominated by sugar maple and basswood trees, and contains thousands of microorganisms, spiders, insects and fungi that all support the unique plant communities in these forests. An amazing diversity of understory plant species are native residents of

In an earthworm-free sugar maple forest, the forest floor can be very thick (up to 10 cm or more) with lighter colored "mineral soil" beneath. There is very little black "top soil" present and most of the decomposition and nutrient cycling occurs in the forest floor, where plants have most of their roots.

After earthworm invasion the forest floor is often rapidly eliminated. Earthworms consume it and mixed it into the mineral soil below creating a thick layer of black "topsoil." While this is desirable in gardens and farm fields, native forest plant species and tree seedlings often do poorly in these dramatically altered soil conditions: the soil is more compacted and nutrient availability has declined as erosion and leaching losses have increased.

the forest floor including trilliums, — the much loved spring flowers — ferns, mosses and dozens of other flowering plants. The duff layer provides protection from predation and extremes in temperature and moisture to the seeds of understory plant species, many of which take up to two years to fully germinate and begin to grow. These understory plants and tree seedlings root almost exclusively in the thick forest floor since this is where most of the available nutrients are found.

When earthworms invade, they can rapidly remove the forest floor, literally

eating the rooting zone out from under the forest plants. In contrast to the effects of earthworms in gardens and farm fields, they lead to increased compaction and soil erosion when they invade hardwood forests, in part because of the removal of the forest floor. Plant roots have a harder time growing in new dense soil, composed mostly of earthworm casts (worm poop), compared to the previously loose and spongy forest floor. Without the protection of the forest floor, plant roots, seeds and germinating seedling are more vulnerable to predation by animals, and to drying and freezing. A few native plant species like jack-in-the-pulpit (*Arisaema triphyllum*) and Pennsylvania sedge (*Carex pensylvanica*) do just fine in these altered conditions, but many native understory plants and tree seedlings don't. As a result, the diversity and abundance of native forest plant communities can decrease dramatically after earthworms invade. In some forests, where once there were carpets of native forest plants such as large-flowered trillium (*Trillium grandiflorum*), nodding trillium (*Trillium cernuum*), bloodroot (*Sanguinaria canadensis*), wild ginger (*Asarum canadense*), large-flowered bellwort (*Uvularia grandiflora*) and sugar maple seedlings (*Acer saccharum*); now there is only bare soil with isolated tufts of Pennsylvania sedge, jack-in-the-pulpit and occasional small shrubs. Non-native plant species such as European buckthorn (*Rhamnus cathartica*), garlic mustard (*Allaria petiolata*) and Japanese honeysuckle (*Lonicera tatarica*) often begin to dominate in these sites either from lack of competition or from disturbed and altered soil conditions to which they may be better adapted than are our native species.

In earthworm-free hardwood forests of the Great Lakes region, the understory plant community is typically composed of a diverse array of wildflowers, ferns, orchids and tree seedlings.

After earthworm invasion, many sites have more exposed bare soil than plants, with only a few remaining plant species. After multiple decades of earthworm invasion, forest understories can become dominated by non-native plant species.

Loss of native species

Research is beginning to emerge that suggests that the invasion of earthworm leads to a cascade of changes in hardwood forest ecosystems. With the loss of the forest floor, many animals such as ground nesting birds, small mammals, amphibians, reptiles, insects and spiders loose their primary habitat and many food sources. While earthworms can be a very good food source for many of these animals, the loss of cover the forest floor used to provide is now gone. With the disappearance of the forest floor, so goes the high quality food and habitat many forest animals relied upon.

In addition, white-tailed deer densities are much higher in modern hardwood forests than they were a century ago, and research has shown that this can contribute to a lack of regeneration of herbaceous understory species including many tree species. The combined effects of deer browsing and earthworm invasion can have a larger effect than either one alone, leading to even more severe impacts on understory plants and tree seedlings. Research suggests that if deer populations are low, some native plant species can recover after earthworms invade, but high deer populations can cause the ultimate extirpation of a native plant species.

EARTHWORMS *in the* ECOSYSTEM

There are four broad ecological groups of earthworms distinguished by both color and size. Knowing which ecological groups of earthworm you have can be valuable to know, even if you do not identify the species, because each group tends to affect the forest differently. Earthworms in different ecological groups have different feeding preferences and burrow systems and this changes the kinds of impacts they have in the forest.

Effects of different ecological groups

Litter-dwelling (*epigeic*) species primarily effect the forest floor. Species that dwell in the surface litter and just below (*epi-endogeic*) also primarily effect the forest floor. Soil dwelling (*endogeic*) species primarily alter the mineral soil horizons, and deep burrowing (*anecic*) species can affect both the forest floor and the mineral soil horizon.

Changes in forest soils, the forest floor and the understory plant communities are much greater when all three ecological groups are present.

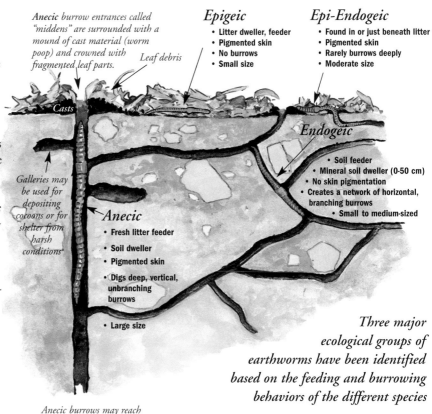

Anecic burrow entrances called "middens" are surrounded with a mound of cast material (worm poop) and crowned with fragmented leaf parts.

Leaf debris

Casts

Galleries may be used for depositing cocoons or for shelter from harsh conditions

Epigeic
- Litter dweller, feeder
- Pigmented skin
- No burrows
- Small size

Epi-Endogeic
- Found in or just beneath litter
- Pigmented skin
- Rarely burrows deeply
- Moderate size

Endogeic
- Soil feeder
- Mineral soil dweller (0-50 cm)
- No skin pigmentation
- Creates a network of horizontal, branching burrows
- Small to medium-sized

Anecic
- Fresh litter feeder
- Soil dweller
- Pigmented skin
- Digs deep, vertical, unbranching burrows
- Large size

Anecic burrows may reach depths up to two meters!

Three major ecological groups of earthworms have been identified based on the feeding and burrowing behaviors of the different species

Epigeic *Litter-Dwelling Species*

Epigeic earthworms are small bodied (1-7 cm) with reddish-brown skin pigmentation which tends to be darker on the back and head so the belly is often more beige in color. Scientists think this pigmentation may provide protection from predators and from ultraviolet rays, to which they are very sensitive.

There are several species in this group that have been identified in the Great Lakes region including *Dendrobaena octaedra, Dendrodrilus rubidus, Eiseniella tetraedra, Eisenia eiseni.* They are strictly litter dwelling species feeding on surface litter, fungi and bacteria found in the forest floor. While they can change the macroinvertebrate and fungal populations with their invasion, they generally do not cause large decreases in the thickness of the forest floor.

This very small species, Dendrobaena octaedra, lives strictly in the litter layer and feeds on fungi and bacteria. As a result, this species has less effect on the forest floor than many other species.

Epi-endogeic *Litter & Surface Dwelling Species*

Epi-endogeic earthworms are pigmented species that feed on organic material or near the surface of the soil. They are generally found in the surface litter or just beneath, on top of the mineral soil, but rarely burrow deeply or form permanent burrows.

Many of these species are used heavily in vermicomposting because they can live in high densities and feed in the interface between fresh litter and soil/compost. Earthworms in this group that have been identified in the Great Lakes region include the European species *Lumbricus rubellus, Eisenia fetida* (also know as *E. foetida*, the Red Wiggler), *Eisenia hortensis, Eisenia veneta* (also known as *Dendrobaena veneta*); the African species *Eudrilus eugeniae*; the South American species *Pontoscolex* species and Asian species *Perionyx excavate*s, and at least two species of *Amynthas*. So far *L. rubellus* and *Amynthas* species are the only two species in this group that have been identified in native habitats of the Great Lakes region, but are likely to survive in warmer regions of the U.S.

This moderately sized species, Lumbricus rubellus, *is commonly sold as fishing bait. It feeds on surface litter and organic material and also grazes on the fungi and bacteria found near plant roots. This species rapidly removes the forest floor when it invades and is associated with big changes in forest soils and plant communities.*

Endogeic *Soil-Dwelling Species*

Adult endogeic earthworms can range from small to large (2-12 cm long as adults), depending on the species, but are identified by their lack of skin pigmentation. As a result, they may appear gray-blue, yellowish, pink or whitish. If their gut is full of dark colored soil, they may appear very dark. Don't be fooled! They lack the red-brown skin pigmentation on the back and head seen with epigeic and anecic species.

Endogeic earthworms live and feed in the mineral soil layers. They ingest mineral soil and digest the organic material and microorganisms found there. They rarely feed at the surface, but may be found under logs and rocks and are often seen at the surface after heavy rains when the surface moisture makes it possible for them to disperse without drying out.

Endogeic species of earthworms form a network of permanent burrows in the mineral soil, down to about 50 cm deep. This allows them to easily access the soil resources. Several species of endogeic earthworms have been identified across the Great Lakes region, three are relatively common.

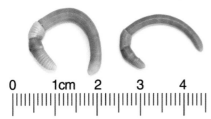

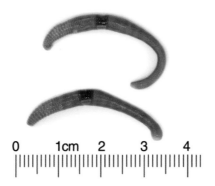

This small, unpigmented species, Aporrectodea rosea, *is common in gardens and agricultural fields. Live specimens can sometimes be distinguished by a very pink head and tail. While common across the region, its populations seem to be more patchily distributed, so it's not clear what their role is in the overall impacts of non-native earthworm invasions.*

This moderately sized, unpigmented species, Octolasion tyrtaeum, *is less common than the* Aporrectodea *species, but is found in patches across the Great Lakes region (along with a closely related species,* Octolasion cyaneum*). Live specimens can sometimes be distinguished by a bright red-orange clitellum.*

This large, unpigmented species, Aporrectodea caliginosa, *is very common in gardens and agricultural fields. It's responsible for much of the mixing of the mineral soil and contributes to the development of the thick layer of dense, black soil after earthworms invade.*

Anecic *Deep Burrowing Species*

Anecic earthworms burrow very deeply (down to two meters) but feed on fresh surface litter which they pull down into their burrows. Anecic earthworm species are very large (8-15 cm long as adults) and strongly pigmented with the same reddish-brown in color seen in epigeic species. These species have the potential to eat huge amounts of litter every year and as a result can have big effects on the forest floor when they invade. In the Great Lakes region, there is only one anecic species of earthworm, the Common Night Crawler (*Lumbricus terrestris*).

This very large, pigmented species, Lumbricus terrestris, is by far the most common earthworm sold for fishing bait across the Great Lakes region. Millions are imported from Canada annually for the fishing industry, but it's an non-native, European species. Night Crawlers can consume all the leaf litter produced in a forest each year, and, by preventing any recovery of the forest floor, contribute to big long-term effects in the forest ecosystem.

```
0    1cm  2    3    4    5    6    7    8    9    10   11
|||||||||||||||||||||||||||||||||||||||||||||||||||||||||||||||||
```

IERAT (Invasive Earthworm Rapid Assessment Tool)

Land managers asked if we could develop a quicker way to assess invasive earthworm impacts so they could more easily include such data collection in their annual surveys. This led to the development of the IERAT, which uses a visual assessment of the forest floor to assign one of five classifications. These indicate the stage of earthworm invasion, level of ecological impact and the associated earthworms most likely present. Here are the classifications and their visual indicators:

Classification 1: Earthworm-Free

The forest floor (see illustration at right) is fully intact and has three recognizable layers (the *Oi, Oe, Oa* horizons), fine plant roots, and white fungi filaments are present in the forest floor layers. No earthworms or earthworm casts are present in the forest floor or mineral soil beneath.

Especially profuse are the macroinvertebrates: the insects, spiders, slugs, etc. that are large enough to see without magnification and have no backbone (i.e. invertebrate). They are reliant on a thick duff layer for protection from desiccation, temperature swings and predators.

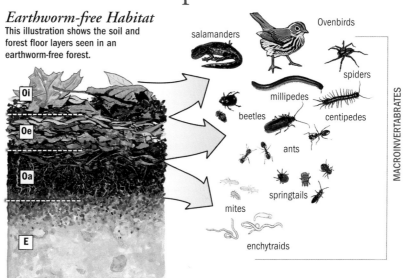

Earthworm-free Habitat
This illustration shows the soil and forest floor layers seen in an earthworm-free forest.

Oi Horizon: *whole, dry and fresh leaves and organic materials from most recent autumn*
Oe Horizon: *fragmented, partially decomposed leaves and other organic material over one year old*
Oa Horizon: *very decomposed organic material, "peat-like" consistency, well colonized by fine roots*
E Horizon: *the mineral soil beneath an intact organic layer where the very top is only slightly darker than the unaltered soil below.*

In turn, they serve as prey for vertebrate species such as small mammals, birds, reptiles and amphibians.

Classification 2: Minimally Impacted

The *Oi* and *Oe* are intact, but the *Oa* horizons is only present in patches and may be slightly mixed with mineral soil and very small castings. Some fine roots and fungi filaments are still present in the forest floor, but may not be as abundant. Small epigeic earthworms (see page 8) are present in the forest floor. No large surface castings or *Lumbricus terrestris* middens are present (see illustration below).

Classification 3: Moderately Impacted

The *Oi* horizon is present throughout the growing season. The *Oe* horizon is greatly reduced, but still detectable. The *Oa* horizons is gone, along with the fine roots and fungi filaments typically associated with this horizon. Small to large epigeic and epi-endogeic earthworms (see page 8) may be detectable in the remaining forest floor, at the surface of the mineral soil beneath the forest floor. No large surface castings or *Lumbricus terrestris* middens are present, however, earthworm casts at the mineral soil surface can be abundant. Less than 50% of the top few inches of mineral soil is made up of earthworm cast material.

*Middens are distinctive piles of cast and leaf material at the openings of nightcrawler (*Lumbricus terrestris*) burrows*

Midden

Classification 4: Substantially Impacted

The *Oi* horizon is present throughout most of the growing season, but may be reduced by the end of fall. The *Oe* and *Oa* horizons are absent, as are fine roots and fungi filaments typically associated with these horizons. Earthworm casts at the mineral soil surface are abundant and could be large, but *Lumbricus terrestris* middens are absent or rare (less 2 middens per square meter). More than 50% of the top few inches of mineral soil is made up of earthworm cast material.

Large surface castings

Classification 5: heavily impacted

The *Oi* horizon is present at the beginning of the growing season, but generally gone by mid-summer, leaving large patches of bare mineral soil with no leaf litter on top. The *Oe* and *Oa* horizons are absent. Earthworm casts at the mineral soil surface are very abundant, as are large surface castings and *Lumbricus ter-*

Heavily Earthworm-impacted Habitat

This illustration shows some of the changes in the animal communities, from birds to tiny insects.

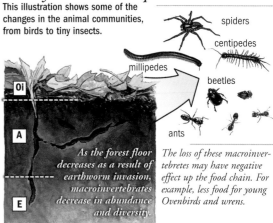

spiders

centipedes

millipedes

beetles

ants

As the forest floor decreases as a result of earthworm invasion, macroinvertebrates decrease in abundance and diversity.

The loss of these macroinvertebretes may have negative effect up the food chain. For example, less food for young Ovenbirds and wrens.

Oi Horizon: *whole, dry and fresh leaves and organic materials from most recent autumn*

The A Horizon: *(not present in earthworm-free soils) a thick, black, compacted layer of mineral soil created by earthworms when they consume the Oe and Oa horizons and mix it with the E horizon.*

restris middens (more than 2 middens per square meter). More than 50% of the top few inches of mineral soil is made up of earthworm cast material.

The IERAT is a simple tool that can be used by land mangers and citizen scientists including educators, private land owners and citizen groups. Results generated using the IERAT can be used to direct land managers decisions regarding where to more intensively sample earthworm populations and to identify minimally impacted areas that may require special protection. Contributing your locally collected data to our growing database on earthworm invasion status will help direct future research and conservations efforts across the region.

IERAT Training Sessions

A short (2-hour) field training session is essential for accurate and efficient use of the IERAT, and for ensuring that data are consistent across different surveyors.

We conduct training sessions in northern Minnesota and northern Wisconsin throughout the summer season and at the request of interested user groups. To inquire about training sessions or to ask questions about the IERAT or earthworm invasions, please contact:
greatlakeswormwatch@gmail.com

HOW DO EARTHWORMS AFFECT ANIMALS IN THE FOREST?

Ovenbird/Thrushes: Fewer Ovenbirds and Hermit Thrushes are found at earthworm-invaded sites compared to earthworm-free sites. The density of Ovenbird nests was also much lower in earthworm-invaded sites. These nests were much more likely to be predated upon if they were placed in habitat that had been altered by earthworms (for example, where a diverse plant community had been replaced by extensive sedge carpets and where the litter layer was greatly reduced).

Ovenbird

Salamanders: Blue-spotted salamanders produce more young in forests with earthworms, but juvenile salamanders are too small to eat earthworms. Because the tiny forest floor insects that juvenile salamanders need are lost with the forest floor when earthworms invade, the salamander population as a whole declines. Declines in forest floor insects — the base of the food web — could lead to declines in other species as well.

Blue-spotted Salamander

Macroinvertebrates: These are the enchytraids, mites, springtails, ants, beetles, centipedes, millipedes, and spiders that are large enough to see without magnification and have no backbone (i.e. invertebrate). As the forest floor decreases as a result of earthworm invasion, macroinvertebrates decrease in abundance and in the diversity of species. These species are reliant on a thick duff layer for protection from desiccation, temperature swings and as refuge from predators. The loss of these macroinvertebretes may have negative effects up the food chain. For example, less food remains for young Ovenbirds and amphibians which may contribute further to their decline.

Grass spider

NOTE: none of the macroinvertebrates are exclusive to a particular layer of the intact forest floor, but require and move through all layers, therefore a decrease in overall thickness and the loss of different layers leads to overall declines in all these species.

EARTHWORM INTERNAL ANATOMY

Earthworms all have the structure of a long cylindrical tube, divided into a series of segments that compartmentalize the body.

Earthworms eat by expanding their mouth to engulf their food. Different species feed on different things, large species such as the common nightcrawler (*Lumbricus terrestris*) eat fresh litter while small litter dwelling species and soil dwelling species engulf fragmented organic material and any associated soil, fungi and bacteria.

Their hearts are really just muscular swellings that pump blood through their bodies. They have no lungs so they "breathe" via gas exchange through the skin (that's why they need to stay moist) and the hearts keep the blood moving along with any dissolved gasses (i.e. oxygen, carbon dioxide). The myth that cutting an earthworm in half will produce two worms is half true: the part with the hearts (the head) can grow a new tail, but the tail cannot grow a new head

Earthworms have very primitive nervous systems. Their "brain" is more accurately referred to as the "cerebral ganglion," made up of a large cluster of nerve cells in the head which connects to ventral nerve cord which runs the length of the body. Earthworms have no eyes but can sense light through specialized cells in their skin. Similarly they can sense vibrations, which is why driving a stick or rod into the ground and then hitting or bowing it to create vibrations in the soil can cause them to come to the surface, often called "grunting" or "fiddling."

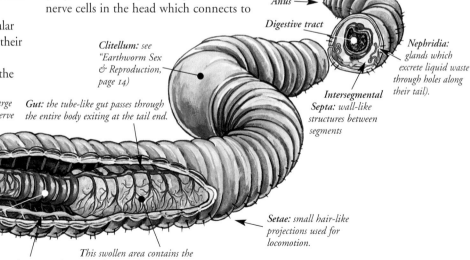

Anus →

Digestive tract

Clitellum: *see "Earthworm Sex & Reproduction, page 14)*

Nephridia: *glands which excrete liquid waste through holes along their tail).*

Intersegmental Septa: *wall-like structures between segments*

Brain: *("cerebral ganglion") consists of a large cluster of nerve cells connected to ventral nerve cord which runs the length of the body.*

Gut: *the tube-like gut passes through the entire body exiting at the tail end.*

Mouth *expands to engulf food.*

Setae: *small hair-like projections used for locomotion.*

Hearts: *are a set of typically five muscular swellings that pump blood through their bodies.*

Ventral nerve cord

This swollen area contains the **crop & gizzard.**

The earthworm digestive system is little more than a tube with specialized sections for grinding their food (the crop & gizzard), extracting water and nutrients (the intestine), excreting liquid waste (the nephridia—holes along their tail), and finally the anus where "cast" material (earthworm poop) is excreted.

Earthworms have small hair-like projections called setae that attach to muscles inside their bodies which they use for locomotion. Different species have different shapes, sizes, color, number and arrangements of their setae which is useful in identifying them. But the basic function is the same.

Earthworms are invertebrates, meaning they do not have bones to provide support for their bodies. The intersegmental septa provide internal structure to help hold all the body parts in place. As a result different segments can have different functions and the placement of some of these features (i.e. male pores, female pores, clitellum, etc.) are very useful in identifying different groups or species of earthworms.

EARTHWORM SEX *and* LIFE CYCLE

Different earthworms use different modes of reproduction. Some are strictly parthenogenetic in that they simply clone themselves, producing cocoons with offspring that contain the exact same genetic make-up as the adult producing them. Others species rely on sexual reproduction. Those who use sexual reproduction may self-fertilize, since they are generally hermaphroditic (have both male and female reproductive parts), or they may reproduce with other earthworms.

Once an earthworm reaches sexual maturity, it develops a clitellum (the swollen band near the head). The same way that snakes shed their skin, earthworms shed a layer of the clitellum. As it slides up over the worm's head it collects eggs and sperm, forming a cocoon that is deposited in the soil or forest floor.

After a period of incubation, the cocoons hatch producing tiny hatchlings that grow into adult earthworms in anywhere from 50 to 75 weeks depending on the species and soil moisture and temperature. Incubation periods can also vary greatly depending the species and habitat conditions.

Many species deposit cocoons in the fall that overwinter to hatch in the spring. Because of this, earthworm populations in the spring are generally dominated by juveniles. More adult earthworms tend to be found in the fall, after they have had the summer to develop. This a good time to sample earthworm populations if you want to identify the species present.

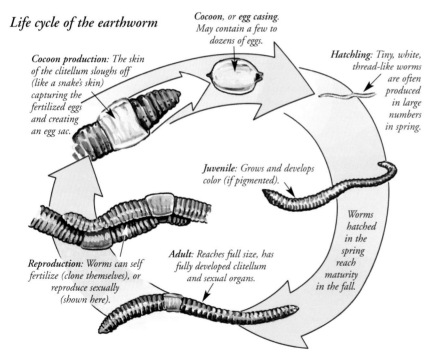

Life cycle of the earthworm

Cocoon, or egg casing. *May contain a few to dozens of eggs.*

Cocoon production: *The skin of the clitellum sloughs off (like a snake's skin) capturing the fertilized eggs and creating an egg sac.*

Hatchling: *Tiny, white, thread-like worms are often produced in large numbers in spring.*

Juvenile: *Grows and develops color (if pigmented).*

Reproduction: *Worms can self fertilize (clone themselves), or reproduce sexually (shown here).*

Adult: *Reaches full size, has fully developed clitellum and sexual organs.*

Worms hatched in the spring reach maturity in the fall.

EARTHWORM EXTERNAL ANATOMY

The **proboscis** (mouth parts) can vary among different earthworm species and may be useful in identification (see page 17).

The presence or absence of skin **pigmentation** (usually brown or red-brown) is an important feature that distinguishes different ecological groups of earthworms (page 12).

The **male pore** is an external opening where sperm is released during reproduction. It is often obvious due to glandular swelling (see page 17).

Earthworms are **segmented.** Various anatomical features used for identification are located on different segments (page 14).

The **clitellum** (klī'telum)—a swollen band-like area near the head end of an earthworm—and its associated features called the tuberculata pubertatis (TP) and genital tumescence (GT) are part of the reproductive system of an earthworm: if an earthworm has a clitellum, it's an adult. If not, it's a juvenile. The position, shape and color of the clitellum and its TP and GT are important features used to identify earthworm species (see pages 14-16).

Segments are separated by an internal membrane called a **septum.**

The **setae** are small hair-like projections on the body of earthworms. The setae are attached to muscles and are used for locomotion. There are several different **setae patterns** which are important features useful in identifying adult and juvenile earthworm (see pages 12-13).

Fresh vs. preserved specimens

Some features seen in fresh specimens are lost when the earthworm is preserved. Conversely, some features are easier to see once the earthworm has been preserved, such as the difference between pigmented and non-pigmented species. Below are some examples seen in fresh (live) earthworms that will help you identify some species.

Eisenia fetida, a pigmented species, also known as the Red Wiggler, has a very distinctive red-yellow banding pattern while the groove between the segments has a mustard-yellow color visible when the earthworm is stretched out a bit.

distinctive red-yellow banding pattern

Eisenia fetida

Lumbricus, a pigmented species, can have a distinctively flattened, triangular tail from muscular movement when the earthworm is crawling. But this characteristic is not always obvious, so its lack doesn't indicate that your earthworm is not in the genus *Lumbricus*.

Lumbricus species

flattened, triangular tail while crawling

Aporrectodea, a pigmented species, often have a very pink nose or tail, may have a whitish band near the head and if the gut is full of darker soil, it maybe visible through the otherwise transparent or translucent non-pigmented skin.

Aporrectodea species

clitellum

whitish band

gut full of darker soil

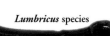

Earthworm pigmentation

The presence or absence of brown or red-brown skin pigmentation is an important feature that distinguishes different ecological groups of earthworms.

Unpigmented earthworms are generally soil dwelling species (endogeic) that feed on soil organic matter and only occasionally come to the surface. While they may have some appearance of "color," especially if their gut is full of dark soil — they do not have brown or red-brown *skin* pigmentation.

Pigmented earthworms are species that feed on surface organic matter. The skin contains a distinctive brown or red-brown pigmentation which is stronger on the head and back (dorsal side) and lighter on the tail and belly (ventral side). Some species are more strongly pigmented than others.

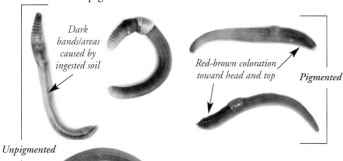

Dark bands/areas caused by ingested soil

Red-brown coloration toward head and top

Pigmented

Unpigmented

Earthworm setae arrangements

The setae are hair-like projections on each segment of an earthworm. They are arranged relative to each other in one of four patterns. In the two most common patterns, setae appear in rows which are arranged in either closely or widely spaced pairs.

Setae and their patterns can sometimes be difficult to see, especially on small or poorly preserved earthworms. The size, thickness and color of the setae itself can also vary among different species. For example, the non-pigmented species often have very small, transparent setae making them hard to see unless viewed with some side light, or they may simply appear as small black dots. The setae are often easiest to see just above or below the clitellum, or near the tip of the tail.

Closely-paired setae:

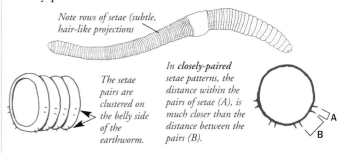

Note rows of setae (subtle, hair-like projections

The setae pairs are clustered on the belly side of the earthworm.

*In **closely-paired** setae patterns, the distance within the pairs of setae (A), is much closer than the distance between the pairs (B).*

Close-ups of "closely-paired" setae seen as tiny black dots.

pair

pair

Widely-paired setae:

*In **widely-paired** setae patterns, the distance within the pairs of setae (A), is only slightly closer than the distance between the pairs (B).*

Note that the pairs of setae are more evenly distributed around the circumference of the earthworms.

Example of a "widely-paired" setae pattern.

Setae pair →

NOTE: The difference between closely- and widely-paired setae includes differences in the amount of space between the two rows of setae in each pair ("A" in illustrations), the distance between the pairs ("B" in illustrations) and the arrangement of the setae around the body.

Separate setae:

In addition to the two "paired setae" arrangements seen in European earthworm species, one species has setae arranged in individual rows evenly spaced around the circumference of the body, referred to as "separate."

*In **separate** setae patterns, the rows of setae are evenly spaced around the circumference of the earthworm and NOT arranged in pairs.*

Note that the setae are more robust, darker and easier to see than other setae patterns.

Setae rows

Bristle-like setae:

In contrast to European species, Asian earthworm species in the genus *Amynthas* have many tiny, bristle-like setae arranged in a row around the circumference of each segment. This pattern is very distinctive.

*In **bristle-like** setae patterns, the setae are arranged in dense rows around each segment.*

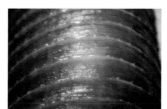

Close-up of "bristle-like" setae seen in the Asian genus Amynthas.

Earthworm segments

Various anatomical features used for identification of earthworm species are often located in different places on the body. Therefore, you may need to count (from mouth to tail) the number of segments to determine the position of different features.

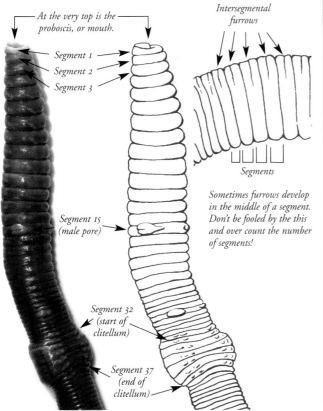

At the very top is the proboscis, or mouth.

Segment 1
Segment 2
Segment 3

Segment 15 (male pore)

Segment 32 (start of clitellum)

Segment 37 (end of clitellum)

Intersegmental furrows

Segments

Sometimes furrows develop in the middle of a segment. Don't be fooled by the this and over count the number of segments!

Earthworm clitellum

The clitellum is a swollen band-like area on adult earthworms that secretes material to make the egg cocoon for reproduction. Its position, shape and color are important features used to identify different earthworm species. There are two distinct shapes:

Saddle-shaped clitellum

The saddle-shaped clitellum is the most common among earthworm species and the one seen on all European species in the family Lumbricidae. In this type, the swollen area of the clitellum wraps around 3/4 of the body, leaving the ventral (belly) side exposed. The ventral edge of the clitellum can be flared or not.

Side view of non-flared saddle clitellum

Side view of flared saddle clitellum

Cross-section of non-flared saddle clitellum

Cross-section of flared saddle clitellum

NOTE: In aged individuals of the European species, the clitellum will lose its swollen appearance and may come to resemble the annular clitellum of the Amynthas species. Other characteristics (such as the lack of the Amynthas's bristle setae) will help you distinguish the Europeans.

Annular clitellum

The annular-shaped clitellum is less common among earthworm species in general, but is seen in the Asian genus *Amynthas*. In this type, the clitellum wraps completely around the body and is less swollen in appearance than in European species.

Side view of annular clitellum

Cross-section of annular clitellum

Earthworm clitellum position

The "position" of the clitellum and its features refers to the segments they occupy when counting from the mouth (see page 14). In this example, the clitellum is on segments 32 through 37.

It is not always obvious where the clitellum starts and ends, but you can usually get within plus or minus one segment. Most of the time you can see the segments within the clitellum, but not always.

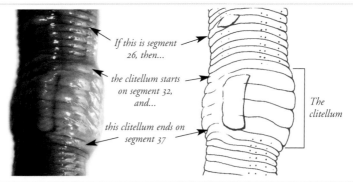

If this is segment 26, then...

the clitellum starts on segment 32, and...

this clitellum ends on segment 37

The clitellum

Earthworm clitellum features

The *tuberculata pubertatis* (TP) and *genital tumescence* (GT) are features associated with the earthworm's clitellum. They can vary in position, shape and color among different species, so are useful in identification. If the earthworm is not fully mature, then these features may not be fully developed and you must take this into account when using these features for identification. The function of the TP and GT are not fully understood, though we assume they play some role in reproduction.

The TP are two slightly swollen and usually differently colored areas on each side of the ventral (belly) surface of the clitellum.

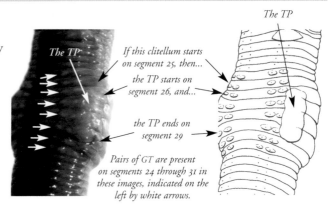

The TP

The TP

If this clitellum starts on segment 25, then...

the TP starts on segment 26, and...

the TP ends on segment 29

Pairs of GT are present on segments 24 through 31 in these images, indicated on the left by white arrows.

The GT are small swollen areas around setae (so they are often paired as are the setae) on each side of the ventral surface of the clitellum. GT may also be seen above or below the clitellum or associate with male and female pores.

The shape and color of the TP and the number and positions of the GT vary quite a bit among species and some species have none. So see the species descriptions for their particular characteristics.

NOTE: GT are often the last feature to develop as the clitellum matures, and the first to disappear.

Male and female pores

Along with the clitellum features, two male pores (for sperm production) and two female pores (for egg production) may develop, one of each on each side, when an earthworm is sexually mature. Some species of earthworms, such as *Lumbricus terrestris*, rely on sexual reproduction and self-fertilization, so male and female pores are often present and easier to see. However, some other species, such as *Dendrobaena octaedra*, rely on parthenogenesis for reproduction, so the male and female pores may be absent.

*Male pores in the European species (*Lumbricidae*), are usually on segment 15. However, in a few species the male pores are on segments 14 or 13, which helps with their identification.*

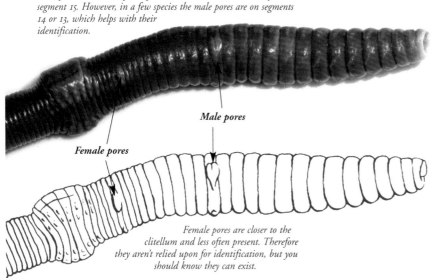

Male pores

Female pores

Female pores are closer to the clitellum and less often present. Therefore they aren't relied upon for identification, but you should know they can exist.

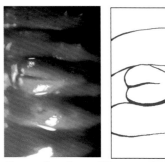

Close-up of a male pore. When an earthworm is sexually mature, the area around the male and female pores swell, making them more obvious. The pore itself is the small slit in the center of the swollen area.

Earthworm proboscis

The proboscis, or mouth part, of an earthworm intersects the first segment in different ways among different earthworm species and can be a helpful feature when confirming an identification. There are four general proboscis arrangements seen. NOTE: During preservation, the mouth can sometimes become deformed making it impossible to distinguish this feature.

2nd segment

1st segment

proboscis

Prolobic and zygolobic are two other mouth types seen in earthworms around the world. Although none of the species in this guide have prolobic or zygolobic mouths, you should be aware of them in case you run across species not presented here.

A prolobic mouth does not divide the first segment.

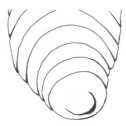

A zygolobic mouth is fused to the first segment so there is no groove separating them.

Epilobic *is the most common mouth type in the family* Lumbricidae, *but not the type seen on species in the genus* Lumbricus. *In an epilobic mouth, the proboscis partially divides the first segment.*

Tanylobic *is the mouth type seen in earthworm species in the genus* Lumbricus. *In a tanylobic mouth, the proboscis completely divides the first segment.*

COLLECTING EARTHWORMS

There are three commonly used methods of collecting earthworms. Depending on your particular objectives, you may choose one sampling method over another or some combination of methods. See our website for more details on sampling methods and study design: www.greatlakeswormwatch.org

Flip & strip method

This method literally involves flipping over logs and rocks, stripping bark off fallen logs and rooting around through leaf litter to see what you find. It is a fun and simple way to get an impression of what kinds of earthworms you may have in a particular site. Please return logs, rocks and bark to their original position.

Hand sample method

You begin by digging a pit, usually at least 35 cm square (14" square) to a depth of at least 15 cm to 30 cm (6"–12"). It's handy to have a tarp laid out next to the pit to put the soil on. Then sift through the soil looking for earthworms. You generally don't need to put the soil through a screen; by simply grabbing handfuls of soil and sifting through it with your fingers you'll find most earthworms present.

The liquid extraction method

This method involves pouring a solution of mustard water on the soil. Mustard is a skin irritant and the earthworms will come to the surface to avoid it, making it easy for you to collect them. The recipe is 40 grams (about 1/3 cup)

Sampling a plot with the liquid extraction method.

ground yellow mustard seed to four liters (about one gallon) of water. Shake to mix well. This is the same powdered yellow mustard you will find in the spice rack in any grocery store. However, it's generally much cheaper to buy it in bulk at the local food co-op.

Four liters of mustard solution will generally sample an area 35 cm x 35 cm square (14" square). Clear away the surface litter in your sample area and a few inches around it. Slowly pour about half of the mustard solution over the entire sample area allowing it to soak in as much as possible. If worms are present and active they should begin coming up almost immediately. If they don't come up right away, wait two minutes or so and then pour again. A forceps is handy for picking the worms up off the surface and some kind of container to put them in until you're done, since they can come up in rapid succession. After a few minutes, and the initial flush of earthworms slows down, pour more of the solution over the sample area. You will probably get another flush. Continue this until the whole jug of mustard juice is used up (2 or 3 pourings). Be sure to wait a few minutes after pouring the last of the liquid to get any slow emergers.

Warning: This is fun! You (or your students) may not want to use the other sampling methods after trying this one.

Preserving earthworms for identification

So, once you have worms, what do you do with them?

Anesthetize the worms in alcohol:
Isopropyl (rubbing alcohol) works great and is cheap and easy to find. Get as much dirt off the worms as possible. Put the worms in the alcohol one at a time so they don't get tangled up into a big mess. After a few seconds, the earthworm will become anesthetized and relax

into a mostly extended position. Place the anesthetized worms into a vial. You can keep the worms in alcohol for the rest of the day (keeping them cool and out of direct sunlight). But don't wait too long or they start to get mushy. Within 24 hours you need to either identify your earthworms or prepare them for longer-term storage using formalin.

Preserving earthworms in formalin:
Formalin is a cellular fixative that will prepare specimens for long-term storage. Place the earthworms from your sample in a vial with a leak-proof lid and cover them in formalin. If you don't have access to vials or formalin contact us at **Great Lakes Worm Watch** for help in acquiring the needed supplies: **www.greatlakeswormwatch.org**

After the earthworms have soaked in formalin for at least 24 hours, they can be transferred to an empty vial and covered with alcohol for long-term storage, that way you can re-use the formalin.

CAUTION: *Formalin is a dangerous chemical and safety precautions must be taken. It should be used only with adult supervision and in a well ventilated area. It should not be inhaled, swallowed or allowed to come in contact with bare skin or eyes. If external contact does occur, wash the area with large amounts of water. If ingested, contact a poison control center immediately. Formalin has been shown to cause cancer in laboratory animals.*

If you are interested in adding your earthworms to the Great Lakes Worm Watch archive, visit our website for information on submitting earthworms for our collection.

ABC'S *of* COMPOSTING *with* EARTHWORMS SAFELY

How does Vermicomposting work?

Vermicomposting is similar to traditional microbial/bacterial composting, except that earthworms are added. The earthworms eat the discarded vegetable matter and convert it into excrement, or cast material, which creates nutrient-rich, finished compost.

The Risk of Vermicomposting

All earthworms in the Great Lakes Region are non-native. Most of the earthworms you know and love are European in origin. Earthworms are beneficial in artificial environments—agriculture and gardens—they can help water to move through the soil and incorporate organic material to make nutrients more available to plants. But earthworms are not good in natural hardwood forests.

Duff is the top layer of thick, spongy, decomposing material found on the forest floors. It is very important for seedling growth and understory vegetation. Once earthworms invade a native forest, they mix the duff layer into the mineral soil, changing the structure, chemistry and biology of living organisms in the soil. Different species of earthworms have different effects on

native forest ecosystems. Red Wigglers (*Eisenia fetida*) are the most common worms used in vermicomposting. They are great compost earthworms for northern climates because they don't survive cold winters and aren't invasive in the Great Lakes region.

ALERT! There are several other species also commonly called Red Wigglers or Red worms such as *Lumbricus rubellus* (sold for bait as Leaf Worms or Beaver Tails) and increasingly, Asian species in the genus *Amynthas*, also called Jumping Worms. These species survive cold winters and can be very detrimental to native forests.

Can I Vermicompost safely?

So what does this mean for the small home vermicomposting operation? By keeping your vermicomposting indoors you will lower the risk of accidental release of earthworms. Use the "worm juice" as plant fertilizer. By filtering the liquid that drains out of your compost bin you will be able to eliminate earthworms and egg cocoons from the "juice" which is full of nutrients. If you are going to use the compost in an outdoor application such as your plant or vegetable garden you can freeze the compost for one week and this will kill earthworms and egg cocoons.

Jumping Worm Alert!

All earthworms in the Great Lakes Region are non-native species brought over from Europe during early colonization of the United States. But there is a new invasive earthworm causing alarm for the native environment. Asian earthworms (genus: *Amynthas*) are becoming a threat in the Great Lakes Region. They are also known as Jumping Worms because they are very active and hyper: very non-traditional earthworm behavior. The *Amythas* species has an extraordinarily high metabolism and these worms can live in very high densities. If they

Amynthas species

Prevent earthworms and their cocoons from being introduced to a natural environment!

become established, their impacts on our native ecosystems could be catastrophic. When you buy "Red Wigglers" for vermicomposting, *Amynthas* earthworms are a common contaminant which can lead to the introduction of this species to the wild. To identify *Amynthas*, or to report a sighting, go to:

www.greatlakeswormwatch.org

What can you do to reduce the spread of non-native earthworms?

• Don't dump vermicomposting earthworms in woods or water. Earthworms don't drown!

• Toss unwanted bait in the trash.

• Tell others about the problems caused by invasive earthworms.

• Do not transport leaves, mulch, compost, or soils from one location to another unless certain there are no earthworms or cocoons present.

• Freeze the vermicompost for at least one week before putting it in your garden or other outside environment. This kills the earthworms and egg cocoons.

BEWARE OF VERMICOMPOSTING EARTHWORMS SOLD ONLINE!

Earthworms that are sold via the internet and shipped interstate are often a mix of species, not identified by species or not correctly identified. They often include Eisenia fetida *(also know as* E. foetida, *the Red Wiggler),* Eisenia hortensis *(European nightcrawler); the African species* Eudrilus eugeniae *(African nightcrawler); the South American species* Pontoscolex spp. *and Asian species* Perionyx excavates, *and at least two species of* Amynthas. *With the exception of* Amynthas spp., *which has been documented in Minnesota and Wisconsin, these vermicompost species have not yet been identified in native habitats of the Great Lakes region, but are known to survive in warmer regions of the U.S.*

EARTHWORM SPECIES

Angle Worm and Canadian Gray Worm Complex
Aporrectodea caliginosa complex (includes *A. caliginosa* and *A. tuberculata*)

These are two of the most common and widely-distributed endogeic (non-pigmented) species across the region. While not usually sold for bait, one or two individuals may be mixed in with a dozen night crawlers or leaf worms bought for bait.

This group contains two very closely related and often difficult to distinguish species: *A. caliginosa* and *A. tuberculata*, which are separated by the patterns of their GT. If the clitellum features are well developed enough to make the distinction, then do so. If not, then these get lumped into a single group called "*A. caliginosa* complex.*"

When the TP are underdeveloped each can appear as two circles or triangles side by side (see bottom illustration at right). As the features develop, the two sections merge to form the notched TP of the full adult. These species can sometimes be confused with *A. trapezoides* which does not have a notched TP.

Other identifying features:
- Non-pigmented (live specimens may have pink nose or tail)
- Male pores on segment 15
- Size ranges between 9-15 cm
- Mouth proboscis is epilobic
- The TP are located on segments 31-33

Clitellum on segments 27-34

Both species have closely-paired setae.

0   1cm   2   3   4   5

Distinguishing between *A. caliginosa* and *A. tuberculata*

Both species are unique in that they have notched TP, but their GT patterns differ:

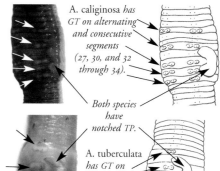

A. caliginosa has GT on alternating and consecutive segments (27, 30, and 32 through 34).

Both species have notched TP.

A. tuberculata has GT on alternating segments only (30, 32, 34).

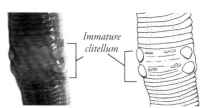

Immature clitellum

Underdeveloped TP can appear as two circles or triangles side by side. As the feature develops, the two sections merge to form the notched TP of the full adult.

Black Head Worm
Aporrectodea longa

This soil-dwelling (endogeic) species is seen across the region and is very common in some agricultural ecosystems, but less common in forests.

A. longa could be confused with other *Aporrectodea* species as well as the larger *Lumbricus* species because it can range from being very unpigmented to having some light pigmentation on the head.

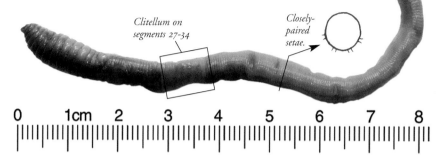

Clitellum on segments 27-34

Closely-paired setae.

Other identifying features:

- Generally non-pigmented, but with some brown pigmentation on the dorsal (back) side of the head, making this a confusing species at times.

- Male pores on segment 15, swelling can extend to 14 and 16

- Size ranges generally between 9-15 cm
- Mouth proboscis is epilobic
- The TP are generally located on segments 32-34

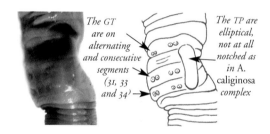

The GT are on alternating and consecutive segments (31, 33 and 34)

The TP are elliptical, not at all notched as in A. caliginosa complex

Angle Worm (Canadian Gray Worm)
Aporrectodea trapezoides

This soil-dwelling (endogeic) species is also common and widely distributed across the region and may be found on the same habitats as *A. caliginosa* and *A. tuberculata*. While not usually sold for bait, one or two individuals may be present in a dozen night crawlers or leaf worms you buy for bait.

A. trapezoides could be confused with other *Aporrectodea* species. It's distinguished from *A. caliginosa* complex because its TP are not notched and from *A. longa* by its lack of pigmentation and the different GT pattern. When the clitellum is very

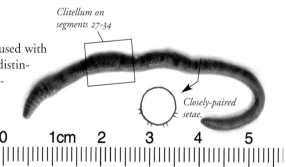

Clitellum on segments 27-34

Closely-paired setae.

immature you may not be able to distinguish among all the *Aporrectodea* species. In this case, you need to call it simply *Aporrectodea* species, indicating that you know the genus, but are unable to determine the species.

Other identifying features:
- Non-pigmented (live specimens may have pink nose or tail)
- Male pores on segment 15
- Size ranges generally between 8-14 cm
- Mouth proboscis is epilobic
- The TP are generally located on segments 31-33

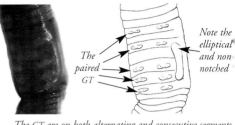

The paired GT

Note the elliptical and non-notched

The GT are on both alternating and consecutive segments (28, 30, and 32 through 34). GT on segment 28 are not clearly visible in the photograph. That's often the case, depending on how well developed the clitellum is.

Rose Worm
Aporrectodea rosea (also *Allolobophora rosea* or *Eisenia rosea*)

This is a very small soil dwelling (endogeic) species. Although less common than the other *Aporrectodea* species with which it can co-habitate, it's found fairly regularly across the region, often in small patches of invaded habitat. Live specimens (see page 11) may have a very pink nose or tail and sometimes have a whitish band (not the clitellum), and these features are lost when they are preserved, so watch for it when sampling! On preserved specimens, the clitellum is often very flared and can obviously stick out from the sides of the earthworm; it's also unique in that the male pore is on segment 14 and not 15, as is the case in most other species.

Other identifying features:
- Non-pigmented but overall color can vary greatly (live specimens may have pink nose or tail)
- Male pores on segment 14, not 15 as in most other species
- GT not present in clitellum, but perhaps with male pores
- Size ranges generally between 2-5 cm, but reported to 8 cm
- Mouth proboscis is epilobic

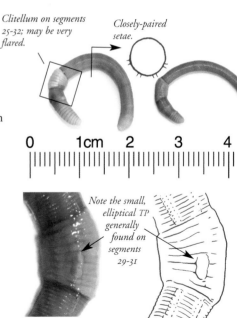

Clitellum on segments 25-32; may be very flared.

Closely-paired setae.

Note the small, elliptical TP generally found on segments 29-31

Swamp Worm (Green Worm)
Allolobophora chlorotica

This soil-dwelling (endogeic) species likes wet, even swampy soil conditions, though it is considered a terrestrial earthworm and not an aquatic worm. It could be confused with other *Aporrectodea* species and *Octolasion* species, though less common than either of these other genera across our region. However, the cluster of features is quite unique on a preserved specimen, especially the TP. Fresh specimens of this species can have a very distinct greenish color that's lost when they're preserved, so be sure to notice this when you're making your collections.

Other identifying features:
- Non-pigmented (live specimens can have a greenish color!)
- Male pores on segment 15
- GT may or may not be present
- Size range is generally 3-7 cm
- Mouth proboscis is epilobic

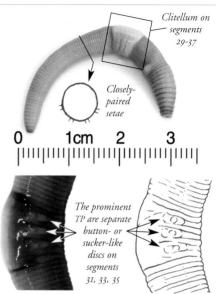

Clitellum on segments 29-37

Closely-paired setae

The prominent TP are separate button- or sucker-like discs on segments 31, 33, 35

Field Worm species
Octolasion tyrtaeum

This moderately-sized soil-dwelling (endogeic) species is much less common than *Aporrectodea* species, but it's found fairly regularly across the region in localized patches. Its parthenogenetic nature may contribute to its more limited distribution pattern. The clitellum can be very orange, reddish or even yellowish in both live and preserved specimens. The light colored TP is a long thin strip on each side of the clitellum and can sometimes been seen with the naked eye on fresh specimens due to the contrast in color with the clitellum. May be confused with *O. cyaneum*.

Other identifying features:
- Non-pigmented; color can vary from gray to bluish or pinkish

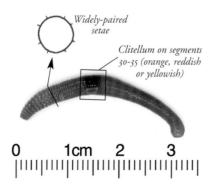

Widely-paired setae

Clitellum on segments 30-35 (orange, reddish or yellowish)

- Widely-paired setae arrangement
- Male pores on segment 15
- GT may or may not be present
- Size ranges general between 3-7 cm, reported up to 18 cm
- Mouth proboscis is epilobic

The linear, oval TP on segments 31-34 contrasts with the color of the clitellum

Field Worm species
Octolasion cyaneum

This moderately sized soil-dwelling (endogeic) species is very similar to *O. tyrtaeum*, but usually distinguishable by clitellum position and TP shape and color. This species is even less commonly seen than is *O. tyrtaeum* but has been documented across the region. In contrast to *O. tyrtaeum*, the clitellum is generally beige or yellowish in live and preserved specimens, though it can have an orange or reddish tone.

Other identifying features:
- Non-pigmented, lacks the red-brown of "pigmented" species
- Widely-paired setae arrangement
- Male pores on segment 15
- Size ranges general between 3-7 cm, reported up to 18 cm
- Mouth proboscis is epilobic

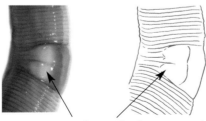

TP on segments 30-33 has a puckered appearance and contrasts with the color of the clitellum. GT may or may not be present.

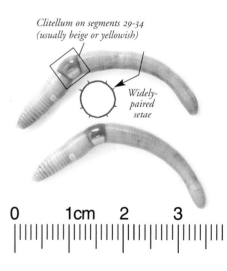

Clitellum on segments 29-34 (usually beige or yellowish)

Widely-paired setae

0   1cm   2   3

Small Leaf Worm
Dendrobaena octaedra

This very small, strictly litter-dwelling (epigeic) species appears to be the most common and widespread of the European species in North America and globally. It is often the first to colonize a previously earthworm-free site. It is strictly parthenogenetic (reproduces by cloning itself). Its cocoons can tolerate amazingly low temperatures, allowing it to colonize areas with more extreme climates than many other species of earthworms. *O. tyrtaeum* can also tolerate more acidic conditions than many other species so it is found in conifer dominated forests as well as hardwood forests. It feeds primarily on fungi and microorganism in the surface litter layer, so when the litter layer is completely removed by other earthworms, this species declines in abundance.

D. octaedra is one of the few species that can readily be identified as a juvenile due to its unique setae pattern.

At first glance it can be confused with *Dendrodrilus rubidus.*

Other identifying features:
- Strongly pigmented, red to dark red-brown
- Male pores on segment 15, if present

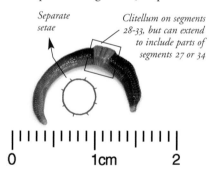

Separate setae

Clitellum on segments 28-33, but can extend to include parts of segments 27 or 34

- GT not present
- Size ranges generally between 1-3 cm, reported up to 6 cm
- Mouth proboscis is epilobic

TP are linear thread-like areas of swelling along the edge of the clitellum, often difficult to see, usually on segments 31-33

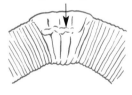

Small Litter Worm
Dendrodrilus rubidus

This very small strictly litter-dwelling (epigeic) species is very similar in habitat and ecology to *D. octaedra* but is distinguishable by its setae pattern, less strong pigmentation and other features. Although it is much less common than *D. octaedra*, they can be found in the same habitats and it is well documented across the region.

Other identifying features:

- Pigmented on back of head and tail with less on the belly

- GT not present

- Size ranges generally between 2-5 cm, reported up to 9 cm

- Mouth proboscis is epilobic

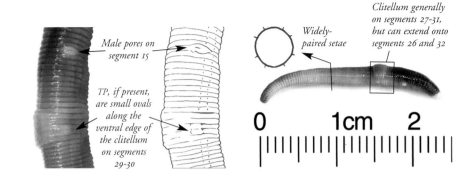

Male pores on segment 15

TP, if present, are small ovals along the ventral edge of the clitellum on segments 29-30

Widely-paired setae

Clitellum generally on segments 27-31, but can extend onto segments 26 and 32

0   1cm   2

Night Crawler (Canadian Crawler, Dew Worm)
Lumbricus terrestris

This very large, deep-burrowing (anecic) species is extremely common across the North America and is perhaps the most commonly sold earthworm used for fishing bait. It is the only very large pigmented species in the Great Lakes region so can be readily identified as an adult. However, as a juvenile without a clitellum, it is indistinguishable from *L. rubellus*. Therefore all juveniles can only be identified as "*Lumbricus* juvenile," indicating that you know the genus, but cannot identify the species. Also, watch for the flattened tail that is indicative of this genus on live specimens: see page 11.

Clitellum on segments 32-37, may extend to 31

Closely-paired setae.

0   1cm   2   3   4   5   6   7   8   9   10   1

Other identifying features:

- Strongly red-brown pigmented on the back with some purple iridescence, paler yellow on the belly

- Male pores prominent on segment 15, swelling can extend to segments 14 and 16

- GT may be present in the clitellum and elsewhere

- Size ranges generally between 9-15 cm, reported to 30 cm

- Mouth proboscis is tanylobic

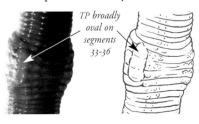

TP broadly oval on segments 33-36

Leaf Worm (Beaver Tail)
Lumbricus rubellus

This moderately-sized, surface-dwelling (epi-endogeic) species is extremely common across the region and often sold for fishing bait. It closely resembles *L. terrestris*, but as an adult it's about half the size and has a different clitellum position. As a juvenile, it's indistinguishable from *L. terrestris*. Therefore, all juveniles can only be identified as "*Lumbricus* juvenile." Also, watch for the flattened tail that is indicative of this genus on live specimens (see page 11). *NOTE: Some identification keys distinguish* L. castaneus *from* L. rubellus *by its smaller size and lack of GT in the clitellum. However, these characteristics are unreliable and the two species are not separated here.*

Other identifying features:
- Strongly red-brown pigmented on the back with some purple iridescence, paler yellow on the belly
- Male pores are inconspicuous, but if visible, on segment 15
- GT may or may not be present
- Size ranges generally between 5-10 cm, but reported to 15 cm
- Mouth proboscis is tanylobic

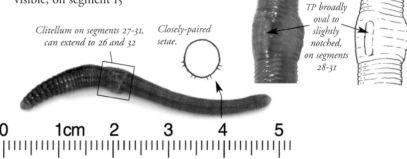

Clitellum on segments 27-31, can extend to 26 and 32

Closely-paired setae.

TP broadly oval to slightly notched, on segments 28-31

Small Brown-nosed Litter Worm
Eiseniella tetraedra

This very small, strictly litter-dwelling (epigeic) species has only been documented in a few location across the Great Lakes region. It is hard to say why they are in so few places, especially when those places are separated by hundreds of miles! It is also a parthenogenetic species that at first glance may be confused with *D. octaedra*, *D. rubidus* or *L. rubellus*. Its features are quite unique, especially the positions of the clitellum and the male pores.

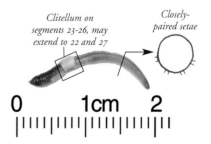

Clitellum on segments 23-26, may extend to 22 and 27

Closely-paired setae

Other identifying features:

- Strongly pigmented dark brown on back with a more golden yellow belly
- Male pores on segment 13
- GT not typically present

- Size range generally between 2-6 cm
- Mouth proboscis is epilobic

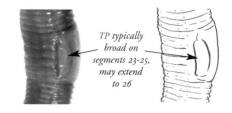

TP typically broad on segments 23-25, may extend to 26

Red Wiggler (Compost Worm)

Eisenia fetida (also known as *E. foetida*)

This moderately-sized surface-dwelling (epigeic) species is the most traditional "compost worm" due to its high metabolism and the ability to live in very high densities. However, it does not appear to survive cold winters outside a compost pile, so has not been documented in natural habitats in the Great Lakes region. That said, it is one to watch for, just in case! One of its most distinctive features, only found on fresh specimens, is the yellow coloration in the groove between the segments giving this species a banded look when stretched out. This feature is lost when preserved, so look for it on live specimens before you preserve them (see page 11).

Other identifying features:

- Strongly red pigmented on the back (dorsal-side)
- Male pores on segment 15
- GT may be present on segments 24-32
- Size ranges generally between 3-13 cm
- Mouth proboscis is epilobic

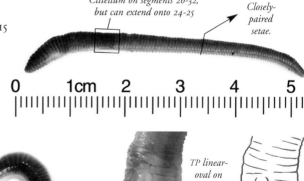

Clitellum on segments 26-32, but can extend onto 24-25

Closely-paired setae.

0   1cm   2   3   4   5

TP linear-oval on segments 28-30, but can extend to segments 27 to 31

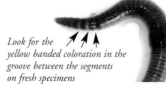

Look for the yellow banded coloration in the groove between the segments on fresh specimens

Brown Litter Worm
Eisenia eiseni (also known as *Lumbricus eiseni*)

This very small, strictly litter-dwelling (epigeic) species has only been documented in a few location across the region (Found once in the belly of a snake!). At first glance this species may be confused with *D. octaedra*, *D. rubidus*, or *E. tetraedra*.

Other identifying features:
- Strongly red-brown pigmented on the back, less on the belly
- TP are absent
- GT may or may not be present
- Size ranges between 3-6 cm
- Mouth proboscis is epilobic

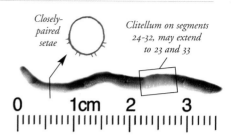

Closely-paired setae

Clitellum on segments 24-32, may extend to 23 and 33

0   1cm   2   3

Jumpers (Jumping Worms)
Amynthas species

This Asian genus is a relatively new non-native earthworm in our region. As a large-bodied surface-dwelling (epi-endogeic) species with a very high metabolism that survives at extremely high densities, it is increasingly sold as a compost worm. It's also often found as a contaminant in batches of red wigglers, but unlike *E. fetida*, it has the potential to survive in more northern habitats. This causes concern that it might become more widespread. It is currently spreading across the eastern Great Lakes region and localized spots in the western Great Lakes region, often via compost and mulch. **Please check if you are bringing either of these materials in from an outside source.**

Most species in this genus are not distinguishable without dissection, which we won't get into here. ***Please report this genus to us if you encounter it!***

The bristle-like setae pattern and wild behavior associated with this genus make it easy to identify. It gets its common name from the way it can "jump" around, in a very unworm-like way.

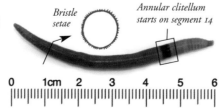

Bristle setae

Annular clitellum starts on segment 14

0   1cm   2   3   4   5   6

LOOK-ALIKE ALERT

A new species with annular clitellum and setae in a row of bristles around each segment, Perionyx excavates *(page 39), has been identified that could be confused with* Amynthas. *The best way to distinguish adults is by the presence of distinctive male pores below the clitellum in* Perionyx excavates, *where* Amynthas *has no obvious pores. Juveniles of these two species may not be distinguishable."*

Other identifying features:
- Different species can be either light or dark colored, but they all lack the contrast between the pigmented back and unpigmented belly of the European pigmented species

- No TP or GT as in the European species
- Size can range between 4–20 cm
- Nose and tail are more pointed than most European species

Unlike European species, Amynthas has a smooth clitellum which encircles the entire body. The clitellum has no other features such as TP or GT found on the European worms.

Super Red
Eisenia hortensis and *Eisenia veneta*

These two species are exceedingly similar in features but differ in mature size where *E. veneta* (also known as *Dendrobaena veneta*) is the larger of the two at 5-15 cm in length while adult *E. hortensis* are 3-7 cm in length with a slightly thicker body above the clitellum. These epi-endogeic species are used for vermicomposting and is often referred to as the "Super Red." They have not been found documented in natural habitats of the Great Lakes Region. Both might be confused with *Eisenia fetida*, the classic Red Wiggler, except that *E. fetida* has closely paired setae.

Other identifying features:
- Color variable, rosy to reddish purple primarily on the head in front of the clitellum, otherwise whitish-yellow below
- Male pores on segment 15
- TP and GT not obvious or reliable features
- Size ranges from 3-7 cm for *E. hortensis*
- Size range from 5-15 cm for *E. veneta*
- Mouth is epilobic to tanylobic

Clitellum on segment 27-33 but can extend onto 26.

Widely paired setae.

0   1cm   2   3   4   5

African Nightcrawler
Eudrilus eugeniae

Known as the African Night Crawler and indigenous to Western Africa. This epi-endogeic species is sold and used for fishing bait and vermicomposting. Because of the annular clitellum, at first glance it can easily be confused for an *Amynthas* species. However, it is distinguishable by having closely paired setae compared to the ring of bristles seen on *Amynthas*.

Other identifying features:
- Color light reddish pigmented on the back (dorsal side) and gray on the underside (ventral)
- Annular clitellum with no TP or GT
- Size ranges 9-14 cm
- Mouth apparently epilobic

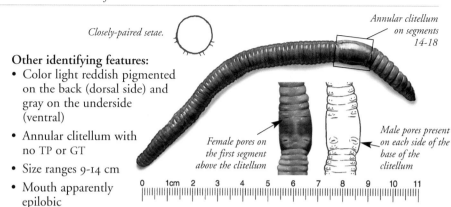

Closely-paired setae.

Annular clitellum on segments 14-18

Female pores on the first segment above the clitellum

Male pores present on each side of the base of the clitellum

Indian Blue Worm
Perionyx excavates

This epi-endogeic species, indigenous to the Himalayan regions of India and Malaysia, appears to be a common contaminant in batches of earthworms sold for vermicomposting, fishing and gardening in the United States. We detected it in batches of Red Wigglers, "fishing worms," African Nightcrawlers and "garden mix" purchased over the internet. This species is also being sold under the name *Pheretima hawayanus* which is an old scientific name for *Amynthas hawayanus*. Because of the annular clitellum and bristle setae pat- tern, it can easily be misidentified as an *Amynthas* spp. However, it is distinguishable by the male pores below the clitellum.

Other identifying features:
- Color can have a blue cast when fresh, changing to gray when preserved
- Annular clitellum with no TP or GT
- Size ranges greatly from 3-18 cm

Male pores closely paired on segment 18 just below the clitellum

Annular clitellum on segments 13-17

Bristled setae

EARTHWORM KEY

This key provides an easy, step-by-step identification for earthworms. Begin at step 1, and follow the key until you reach a species identification. Be sure to double check the identification with the full list of characteristics for that species.

To identify an earthworm to species you generally need an adult with a clitellum. Although most of this guide is dedicated to identifying adults, we provide information on identifying juveniles when possible.

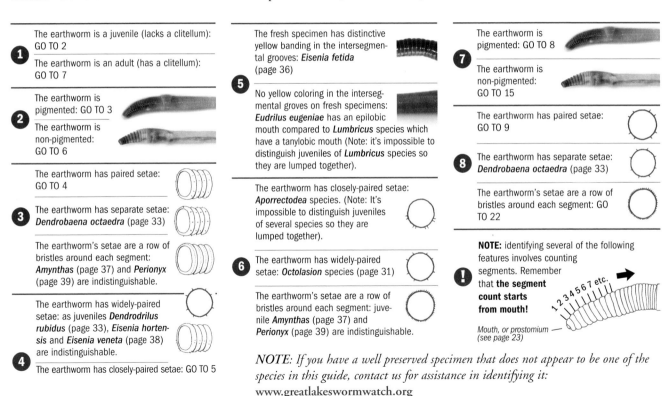

1
The earthworm is a juvenile (lacks a clitellum): GO TO 2

The earthworm is an adult (has a clitellum): GO TO 7

2
The earthworm is pigmented: GO TO 3

The earthworm is non-pigmented: GO TO 6

3
The earthworm has paired setae: GO TO 4

The earthworm has separate setae: *Dendrobaena octaedra* (page 33)

The earthworm's setae are a row of bristles around each segment: *Amynthas* (page 37) and *Perionyx* (page 39) are indistinguishable.

4
The earthworm has widely-paired setae: as juveniles *Dendrodrilus rubidus* (page 33), *Eisenia hortensis* and *Eisenia veneta* (page 38) are indistinguishable.

The earthworm has closely-paired setae: GO TO 5

5
The fresh specimen has distinctive yellow banding in the intersegmental grooves: *Eisenia fetida* (page 36)

No yellow coloring in the intersegmental groves on fresh specimens: *Eudrilus eugeniae* has an epiloboic mouth compared to *Lumbricus* species which have a tanylobic mouth (Note: it's impossible to distinguish juveniles of *Lumbricus* species so they are lumped together).

6
The earthworm has closely-paired setae: *Aporrectodea* species. (Note: It's impossible to distinguish juveniles of several species so they are lumped together).

The earthworm has widely-paired setae: *Octolasion* species (page 31)

The earthworm's setae are a row of bristles around each segment: juvenile *Amynthas* (page 37) and *Perionyx* (page 39) are indistinguishable.

7
The earthworm is pigmented: GO TO 8

The earthworm is non-pigmented: GO TO 15

8
The earthworm has paired setae: GO TO 9

The earthworm has separate setae: *Dendrobaena octaedra* (page 33)

The earthworm's setae are a row of bristles around each segment: GO TO 22

! **NOTE:** identifying several of the following features involves counting segments. Remember that **the segment count starts from mouth!**

Mouth, or prostomium (see page 23)

NOTE: If you have a well preserved specimen that does not appear to be one of the species in this guide, contact us for assistance in identifying it:
www.greatlakeswormwatch.org

9 The earthworm has widely-paired setae: *Dendrodrilus rubidus* clitellum is on segments 27-31 (page 33) compared to *Eisenia hortensis* and *Eisenia veneta* where the clitellum is on segments 26-32 (page 38).

The earthworm has closely-paired setae: GO TO 10

10 The saddle-shaped clitellum starts before segment 25: GO TO 11
Saddle-shaped
Less than 25 segments

The saddle-shaped clitellum starts after segment 25: GO TO 12
More than 25 segments

The clitellum is annular: *Eudrilus eugeniae* (page 39)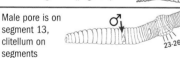

11 Male pore is on segment 13, clitellum on segments 23–26: *Eiseniella tetraedra* (page 35)
23-26

No male pore on segment 13, clitellum on segments 24-32: *Eisenia eiseni* (page 37)

---

12 The clitellum starts on segment 32: *Lumbricus terrestris* (page 34)

The clitellum starts before segment 30: GO TO 13

13 The clitellum starts on segments 26 or 27 and there's no obvious yellow color in the intersegmental grooves: GO TO 14

The clitellum starts on segments 24, 25 or 26 and there is obvious yellow color in the intersegmental grooves: *Eisenia fetida* (page 36)

14 The clitellum is on segments 27 (or 26) through 32 and the worm is darkly pigmented: *Lumbricus rubellus* (page 35)

The clitellum is on segments 27 through 34 and the worm is only slightly pigmented: *Aporrectodea longa* (page 29)

---

15 The earthworm has widely-paired setae: GO TO 16

The earthworm has closely-paired setae: GO TO 17

The earthworm has an annular clitellum and its setae are a row of bristles around each segment: GO TO 23

---

16 The clitellum is on segments 30-35 (may be orangish in color) with long linear TP on segments 31-34: *Octolasion tyrtaeum* (page 31)

The clitellum is on segments 29-34 (usually beige or yellowish) with wide TP on segments 30-33 and may have a puckered-look: *Octolasion cyaneum* (page 32)

---

17 The clitellum starts on segments 27 or later: GO TO 18

The clitellum is on segments 25-32, maybe noticeably flared: *Aporrectodea rosea* (page 30)
Flared Clitellum

18 The clitellum is on segments 27-34: GO TO 20

The clitellum is on segments 29-37: *Allolobophora chlorotica* (page 31)

The TP is distinctly notched GO TO 20

19 TP is not fully developed, appears as two triangles or circular bumps side by side: *Aporrectodea caliginosa* complex (page 28)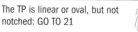

The TP is linear or oval, but not notched: GO TO 21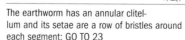

The GT are on alternating segments in clitellum (30, 32, 34): **Aporrectodea tuberculata** (page 28)

20 The GT are on both alternative and consecutive segments in clitellum (27, 30, 32-34): **Aporrectodea caliginosa** (page 28)

On alternating and...

consecutive segments

The GT are on alternative and consecutive segments (28, 30, 32-34) and earthworm has no pigmentation: **Aporrectodea trapezoides** (page 28)

21 The GT are on consecutive on segments (31, 33, 34) and earthworm has light brown pigmentation on the head: **Aporrectodea longa** (page 28)

The earthworm has males pores on section 18, just below the clitellum: **Perionyx excavates** (page 39).

22 The earthworm lacks any obvious male or female pores adjacent to the clitellum: **Amynthas** species (page 37).

INDEX

BIBLIOGRAPHY

This guide is not intended to be used as a taxonomic authority. We relied on other authors for our descriptions of the characteristics of different species. Our taxonomic authorities based their descriptions on careful examination of each species from specimen collections.

Taxonomic Authorities

Reynolds, J.W. 1977. THE EARTHWORMS (LUMBRICIDAE AND SPARGANOPHILIDAE) OF ONTARIO. *Life Sciences Miscellaneous Publications*, Royal Ontario Museum, 100 Queen's Park, Toronto, Canada, M5S 2C6.

Schwert, D.P. 1990. OLIGOCHAETA: LUMBRICIDAE. IN: Dindal, D.L. (editor) SOIL BIOLOGY GUIDE, Pages 341-356. John Wiley & Sons, New York.

James, S.W. 1990. OLIGOCHAETA: MEGASCOLECIDAE AND OTHER EARTHWORMS FROM SOUTHERN AND MIDWESTERN NORTH AMERICA. IN: Dindal, D.L. (editor) SOIL BIOLOGY GUIDE, Pages 379-386. John Wiley & Sons, New York.

General References

Baskin, Y. 2005. HOW CREATURES OF MUD AND DIRT SHAPE OUR WORLD UNDERGROUND, A project of *SCOPE, the Scientific Committee on Problems of the Environment*. Island Press, Shearwater Books, WA

Bohlen, P.J., S. Scheu, C.M. Hale, M.A. McLean, S. Migge, P.M. Groffman, D. Parkinson. 2004. NON-NATIVE INVASIVE EARTHWORMS AS AGENTS OF CHANGE IN NORTHERN TEMPERATE FORESTS. *Frontiers in Ecology and the Environment* 2(8): 427-435.

Callaham, M.A. Jr., G. González, C.M. Hale, L. Heneghan, S.L. Laconic, and X. Zou. In press. POLICY AND MANAGEMENT RESPONSES TO EARTHWORM INVASIONS. *Biological Invasions* 7(6): 1317-1329.

Darwin, C. 1882. THE FORMATION OF VEGETABLE MOULD, THROUGH THE ACTION OF WORMS WITH OBSERVATIONS ON THEIR HABITS. J. Murray, London.

Frelich, L.E., C.M. Hale, S. Scheu, A.R. Holdsworth, L. Heneghan, P.J. Bohlen, and P.B. Reich. 2006. EARTHWORM INVASION INTO PREVIOUSLY EARTHWORM-FREE TEMPERATE AND BOREAL FORESTS. *Biological Invasions* 7(6): 1235-1245.

Gates, G.E. 1966. REQUIEM FOR MEGADRILE UTOPIAS. A CONTRIBUTION TOWARD THE UNDERSTANDING OF THE EARTHWORM FAUNA OF NORTH AMERICA. *Proceedings of the Biological Society*, Washington 79: 239-254.

Gates, G.E. 1982. FAREWELL TO NORTH AMERICAN MEGADRILES. *Megadrilogica* 4(1-2): 12-77.

Hale, C. M., L. E. Frelich, P. B. Reich. 2006. CHANGES IN COLD-TEMPERATE HARDWOOD FOREST UNDERSTORY PLANT COMMUNITIES IN RESPONSE TO INVASION BY EUROPEAN EARTHWORMS. *Ecology* 87(7): 1637-1649.

Hale, C.M., J. Pastor, K. Rusterholz. 1999. COMPARISON OF STRUCTURAL AND COMPOSITIONAL CHARACTERISTICS IN OLD-GROWTH VERSUS MATURE HARDWOOD FORESTS OF MINNESOTA, USA. *Canadian Journal of Forest Research* 29: 1479-1489.

Hale, C.M., L.E. Frelich, P.B. Reich, J. Pastor. 2005. EFFECTS OF EUROPEAN EARTHWORM INVASION ON SOIL CHARACTERISTICS IN NORTHERN HARDWOOD FORESTS OF MINNESOTA, USA. *Ecosystems* 8:911-927.

Hale, C.M., L.E. Frelich, P.B. Reich. 2005. EXOTIC EUROPEAN EARTHWORM INVASION DYNAMICS IN NORTHERN HARDWOOD FORESTS OF MINNESOTA, USA. *Ecological Applications* 15(3):848-860.

Hale, C.M. and G.E. Host. 2005. ASSESSING THE IMPACTS OF EUROPEAN EARTHWORM INVASIONS IN BEECH-MAPLE HARDWOOD AND ASPEN-FIR BOREAL FORESTS OF THE WESTERN GREAT LAKES REGION. *National Park Service Great Lakes Inventory and Monitoring Network Report* GLKN/2005/11.

Hale, C.M., L.E. Frelich, P.B. Reich. 2004. ALLOMETRIC EQUATIONS FOR ESTIMATION OF ASH-FREE DRY MASS FROM LENGTH MEASUREMENTS FOR SELECTED EUROPEAN EARTHWORM SPECIES (LUMBRICIDAE) IN THE WESTERN GREAT LAKES REGION. *American Midland Naturalist* 15(1):179-185.

Hendrix, P.F. (ed.) 1995. EARTHWORM ECOLOGY AND BIOGEOGRAPHY IN NORTH AMERICA, CRC Press, Boca Raton, FL.

Proulx, N. 2003. ECOLOGICAL RISK ASSESSMENT OF NON-INDIGENOUS EARTHWORM SPECIES. Minnesota Department of Natural Resources, 500 Lafayette Rd. St. Paul, MN 55155, Prepared for U.S. Fish and Wildlife Service, International Affairs, Division of Scientific Authority.

Reynolds, J.W., D.R. Linden, C.M. Hale. 2002. THE EARTHWORMS OF MINNESOTA (OLIGOCHAETA: ACANTHODRILIDAE, LUMBRICIDAE AND MEGASCOLECIDAE). *Megadrilogia* 8(12): 86-100.

Smith, F. 1928. AN ACCOUNT OF CHANGES IN THE EARTHWORM FAUNA OF ILLINOIS AND A DESCRIPTION OF ONE NEW SPECIES. *State of Illinois Department of Registration and Education Bulletin* 17(10): 545-550.

Stewart, A. THE EARTH MOVED — ON THE REMARKABLE ACHIEVEMENTS OF EARTHWORMS. Algonquin Books of Chapel Hill, 2004.

Tiunov, A. V., C. M. Hale, A. R. Holdsworth, T. S. Perel. In press. INVASION PATTERNS OF LUMBRICIDAE INTO THE PREVIOUSLY EARTHWORM-FREE AREAS OF NORTH-EASTERN EUROPE AND THE WESTERN GREAT LAKES REGION OF NORTH AMERICA. *Biological Invasions* 7(6): 1223-1234.

Loss, S.R., R.M. Hueffmeier, C.M. Hale, G.E. Host, G.Sjerven, L.E.Frelich. In press. EARTHWORM INVASIONS IN NORTHERN HARDWOOD FORESTS: A RAPID ASSESSMENT METHOD. Natural Areas Journal.

Loss, S.R., R.B. Blair. 2011. REDUCED DENSITY AND NEST SURVIVAL OF GROUND-NESTING SONGBIRDS RELATIVE TO EARTHWORM INVASIONS IN NORTHERN HARDWOOD FORESTS. Conservation Biology 25(4):983-992.

Loss, S.R., G.J.Niemi, R.B.Blair, 2012. INVASIONS OF NON-NATIVE EARTHWORMS RELATED TO POPULATION DECLINES OF GROUND-NESTING SONGBIRDS ACROSS A REGIONAL EXTENT IN NORTHERN HARDWOOD FORESTS OF NORTH AMERICA. Landscape Ecology 27(5):683-696.

Maerz, J.C., V.A. Nuzzo, B. Blossey. 2009. DECLINES IN WOODLAND SALAMANDER ABUNDANCE ASSOCIATED WITH NON-NATIVE EARTHWORM AND PLANT INVASION. Conservation Biology 23(4):975-981.

Migge-Kleian, S., M.A. McLean, J.C. Maerz, L. Heneghan, 2006. THE INFLUENCE OF INVASIVE EARTHWORMS ON INDIGENOUS FAUNA IN ECOSYSTEMS PREVIOUSLY UNINHABITED BY EARTHWORMS. Biological Invasions 8:1275-1285.

Funders and Supporters

Over the years numerous programs and agencies have provided support for research and the development of Great Lakes Worm Watch program including:

Boulder Lake Environmental Learning Center
A program of the Center for Outdoor and Environmental Education, University of Minnesota Duluth

The **Coastal Zone Management Act** and NOAA's **Office of Ocean and Coastal Resource Management**, in cooperation with **Minnesota's Lake Superior Coastal Program**.

The Minnesota Department of Natural Resources
Environmental and Conservation Partnerships Grant Program

Funding for this project was provided by the **Minnesota Environment and Natural Resources Trust Fund** as recommended by the **Legislative-Citizen Commission on Minnesota Resources** (LCCMR).

The National Science Foundation

The Natural Resources Research Institute

The Northeast Regional Sustainable Development Partnership

The University of Minnesota Center for Hardwood Ecology

Further Information

For any inquires, please contact:
Ryan Hueffmeier,
Program Coordinator
greatlakeswormwatch@gmail.com

Or visit our website:
www.greatlakeswormwatch.org

Or call us:
218.720.4310

Or write us:
Great Lakes Worm Watch
Natural Resources Research Institute
University of Minnesota-Duluth
5013 Miller Trunk Highway
Duluth, MN 55811-1442